OCEAN LIFE
UP CLOSE

Bottlenose
Dolphins

by Kari Schuetz

BELLWETHER MEDIA · MINNEAPOLIS, MN

Note to Librarians, Teachers, and Parents:

Blastoff! Readers are carefully developed by literacy experts and combine standards-based content with developmentally appropriate text.

Level 1 provides the most support through repetition of high-frequency words, light text, predictable sentence patterns, and strong visual support.

Level 2 offers early readers a bit more challenge through varied simple sentences, increased text load, and less repetition of high-frequency words.

Level 3 advances early-fluent readers toward fluency through increased text and concept load, less reliance on visuals, longer sentences, and more literary language.

Level 4 builds reading stamina by providing more text per page, increased use of punctuation, greater variation in sentence patterns, and increasingly challenging vocabulary.

Level 5 encourages children to move from "learning to read" to "reading to learn" by providing even more text, varied writing styles, and less familiar topics.

Whichever book is right for your reader, Blastoff! Readers are the perfect books to build confidence and encourage a love of reading that will last a lifetime!

This edition first published in 2017 by Bellwether Media, Inc.

No part of this publication may be reproduced in whole or in part without written permission of the publisher. For information regarding permission, write to Bellwether Media, Inc., Attention: Permissions Department, 5357 Penn Avenue South, Minneapolis, MN 55419.

Library of Congress Cataloging-in-Publication Data

Names: Schuetz, Kari, author.
Title: Bottlenose Dolphins / by Kari Schuetz.
Description: Minneapolis, MN : Bellwether Media, Inc., [2017] | Series:
    Blastoff! Readers. Ocean Life Up Close | Audience: Ages 5-8. | Audience:
    K to grade 3. | Includes bibliographical references and index.
Identifiers: LCCN 2015049955 | ISBN 9781626174139 (hardcover : alk. paper)
Subjects: LCSH: Bottlenose dolphin—Juvenile literature.
Classification: LCC QL737.C432 S4285 2017 | DDC 599.53/3–dc23
LC record available at http://lccn.loc.gov/2015049955

Printed in the United States of America, North Mankato, MN.

Table of Contents

What Are Bottlenose Dolphins?

beak

Bottlenose dolphins are smart and social ocean animals. They are named for their short, rounded beaks.

These dolphins are famous for their noises. They may whistle, click, or squeak!

Common bottlenose dolphins swim
in warm waters all over the world.
A smaller kind stays only in the
Indian and Pacific Oceans.

Home is often near a coast. But some bottlenose dolphins live offshore.

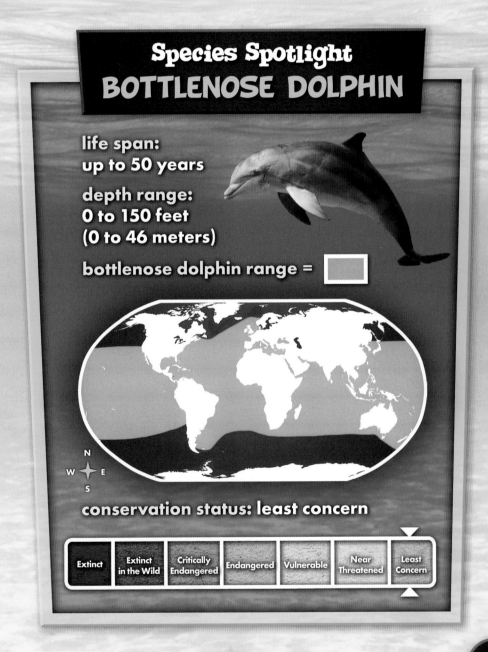

Species Spotlight
BOTTLENOSE DOLPHIN

life span:
up to 50 years

depth range:
0 to 150 feet
(0 to 46 meters)

bottlenose dolphin range =

N
W — E
S

conservation status: **least concern**

Extinct	Extinct in the Wild	Critically Endangered	Endangered	Vulnerable	Near Threatened	Least Concern

Friendly and Fast

Bottlenose dolphins have lasting smiles. Their friendly looks come from their curved mouths.

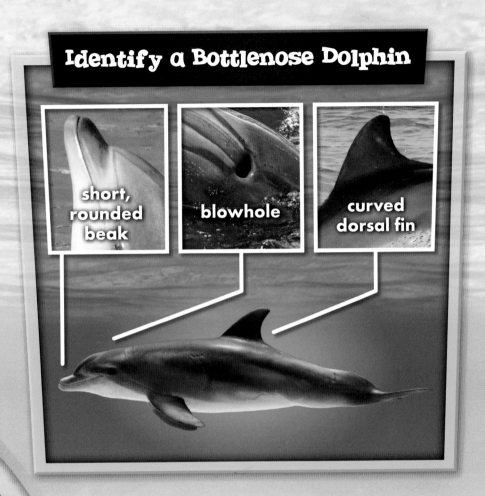

Identify a Bottlenose Dolphin

short, rounded beak

blowhole

curved dorsal fin

To get air, these **mammals** pop their heads above the surface. They breathe through a **blowhole**.

Bottlenose bodies are 6 to 13 feet (2 to 4 meters) long. Adults can weigh more than 1,000 pounds (454 kilograms)!

Bottlenose Dolphin Size

average human

up to 13 feet (4 meters) long

Skin is shaded for hunting and hiding. Gray backs match the dark ocean floor. White stomachs blend with sunlight at the surface.

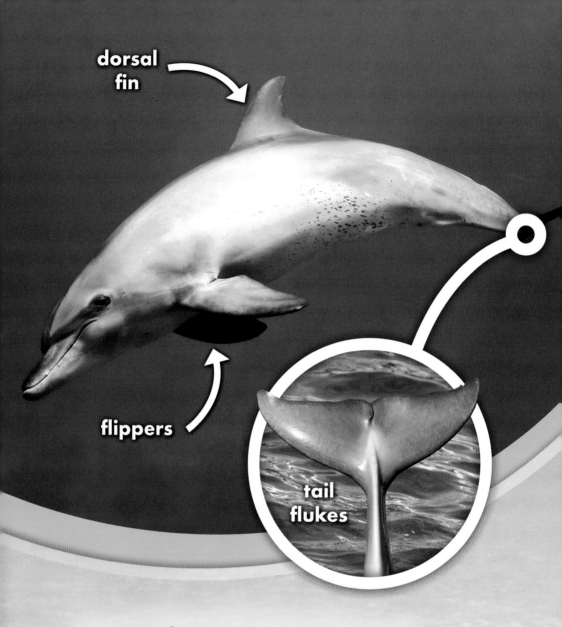

dorsal
fin

flippers

tail
flukes

Large fins help bottlenose
dolphins glide through water.
The curved **dorsal fin** keeps
them balanced.

Tail **flukes** move up and down to push the dolphins forward. Side **flippers** control turns and stops.

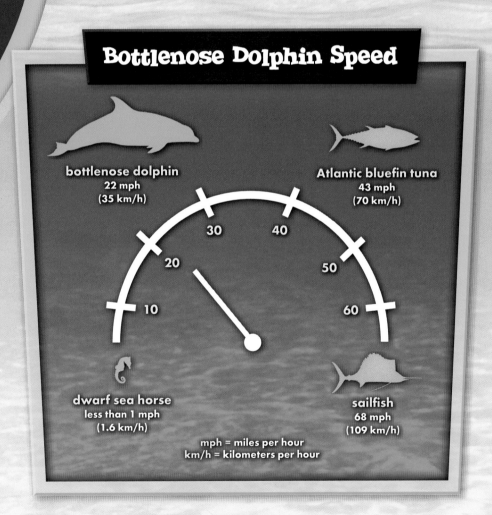

Bottlenose Dolphin Speed

bottlenose dolphin
22 mph
(35 km/h)

Atlantic bluefin tuna
43 mph
(70 km/h)

30   40

20   50

10   60

dwarf sea horse
less than 1 mph
(1.6 km/h)

sailfish
68 mph
(109 km/h)

mph = miles per hour
km/h = kilometers per hour

Catching a Meal

Bottlenose dolphins make clicking noises to find food. The clicks travel through water as **sound waves**.

They can hit other animals and bounce back. The **echoes** tell where **prey** swim. They also warn of **predatory** sharks.

Catch of the Day

Atlantic croakers

flathead mullets

silver perch

To catch dinner, bottlenose dolphins often chase fish toward shore. Sometimes they slap fish with their flukes. This **stuns** the prey!

Then they use their teeth to grab
prey. Finally, they swallow their
meals whole and headfirst!

Life in a Pod

Bottlenose dolphins
live in groups called
pods. Offshore pods
are the largest.

18

Pods travel, hunt, and raise their young together. They use many sounds to talk to one another.

A pod is active a lot of the time. The dolphins chase one another and toss seaweed around.

Sometimes they **breach**. This is a high jump out of the water that ends with a big splash!

Glossary

blowhole—the hole on top of a bottlenose dolphin's head that is used for breathing

breach—to leap out of the water

dorsal fin—the fin on top of a bottlenose dolphin's back

echoes—sounds that repeat over and over after they bounce off a surface

flippers—flat, wide body parts that are used for swimming

flukes—the two halves of a bottlenose dolphin's tail fin

mammals—warm-blooded animals that have backbones and feed their young milk

pods—groups of bottlenose dolphins

predatory—living by hunting other animals for food

prey—animals that are hunted by other animals for food

sound waves—the movements of sounds

stuns—surprises and makes dizzy

To Learn More

AT THE LIBRARY
Hansen, Grace. *Bottlenose Dolphins*. Minneapolis, Minn.: Abdo Kids, 2015.

Spilsbury, Richard and Louise. *Dolphin and Whale Pods*. New York, N.Y.: PowerKids Press, 2013.

Yates, David, and Craig, Juliana, and Isabella Hatkoff. *Hope for Winter: The True Story of a Remarkable Dolphin Friendship*. New York, N.Y.: Scholastic Inc., 2014.

ON THE WEB
Learning more about bottlenose dolphins is as easy as 1, 2, 3.

1. Go to www.factsurfer.com.

2. Enter "bottlenose dolphins" into the search box.

3. Click the "Surf" button and you will see a list of related web sites.

With factsurfer.com, finding more information is just a click away.

Index

The images in this book are reproduced through the courtesy of: Brian J. Skerry/ National Geographic Creative/ Corbis, front cover, p. 20; Shane Gross, pp. 3, 7, 9 (bottom); Tier und Naturfotografie/ SuperStock, pp. 4-5; Andrea Izzotti, p. 5 (top); Anna segeren, p. 5 (center); IDAK, p. 5 (bottom); Dray van Beeck/ Alamy, p. 6; Brandon Bourdages, p. 8; Natali Glado, p. 9 (top left); Sokolov Alexey, p. 9 (top center); Steve Noakes, p. 9 (top right); vkilikov, p. 11; PhotoStock-Israel/ Alamy, p. 12 (top); Dmitri Ma, p. 12 (bottom); SEFSC Pascagoula Laboratory/ Wikipedia, p. 15 (top left, top right); Roberto Pillon/ Wikipedia, p. 15 (top center); Minden Pictures/ SuperStock, p. 15 (bottom); Karen van der Zijden/ Alamy, pp. 16, 17; Flip Nicklin/ Minden Pictures/ SuperStock/ Corbis, pp. 18, 19; Jürgen & Christine Sohns/ Glow Images, p. 21.